The

Senior's Guide
to eBay®

Browsing, Buying and Selling

Check out these other great titles in the Senior's Guide Series!

The
Senior's Guide
to Digital Photography

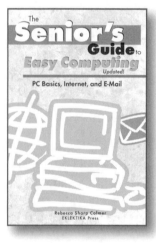

The
Senior's Guide
to Easy Computing

The
Senior's Guide
to Dating (Again)

The

Senior's Guide
to eBay®

Browsing, Buying and Selling

By Rebecca Sharp Colmer
and
Todd M. Thomas

EKLEKTIKA PRESS
Chelsea, Michigan

To Flip

"Business goes where it is invited and stays
where it is well-treated."
American Proverb

ACKNOWLEDGMENTS

Thanks to:

Kim, Abigail, and Ben; once again you've given me time to do my thing.

Thanks to:

Flip Colmer, you're the best.

Thanks to:

Brian Van Geest, Gloria Miller, Tim Zulewski, Vicki Kellogg

Special Thanks to:

All the Seniors.

Table of Contents

Table of Contents

Table of Contents

Table of Contents

Table of Contents

Table of Contents

Part 8 — Selling On eBay 157

Table of Contents

DISCLAIMER

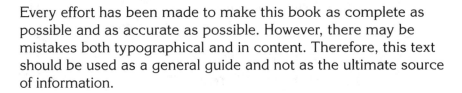

Every effort has been made to make this book as complete as possible and as accurate as possible. However, there may be mistakes both typographical and in content. Therefore, this text should be used as a general guide and not as the ultimate source of information.

WE WANT TO HEAR FROM YOU!

Send us an email with stories about your eBay experiences. What's the best deal you have found? What's the wildest item you have found? Who knows, we may post it on our web site.

Also feel free to email us your questions. We'll be glad to help if we can.

Visit our web site: www.theseniorsguide.com and send us an email.

You can always contact us the old fashioned way:

The Senior's Guide
EKLEKTIKA Press
P. O. Box 157
Chelsea, MI 48118

GETTING THE MOST FROM THIS BOOK

We wrote this book for people of all eBay experience levels, but we do not assume that everyone has been to the eBay web site.

If you are new to eBay, start with Part 1 and work your way through the book. If you are already an eBay member you may want to skip to Part 3 or Part 8 depending if you want to learn more about buying or selling items.

As with any computer-related book, we adopted certain text styles to represent different things:

- Web links are listed with an underline, ex. www.eBay.com.
- Links within the eBay web site are shown as underlined words, ex. services.
- Button labels are written in bold text, ex. **OK**, **Submit**.

eBay is a dynamic web site and changes often. The information we have provided was accurate at the time of publication. Although the eBay site may change, the concepts provided should not.

PART 1

Welcome to eBay!

Congratulations! By purchasing this book you have taken the first step in joining the eBay revolution. You will be shopping and buying with confidence in no time once you have read this book and surfed around on eBay.

In this Part we provide an overview of eBay, how it works, and what you can buy and sell. This introduction prepares you for the rest of the book.

WHAT IS EBAY?

eBay is an international community of buyers and sellers linked together via the Internet. People from all over the globe use eBay to buy and sell merchandise and services. Some people even earn a living as eBay sellers.

eBay started as a simple Internet auction site. However, over the years it has grown into a powerful and dynamic electronic marketplace. In fact, some businesses center solely around buying and selling on eBay.

eBay is an Internet commerce site with most transactions occurring electronically over the Internet. Buyers can pay sellers with checks or other traditional methods. However, more often than not, money changes hands electronically by direct bank transfers or credit card transactions.

As an eBay buyer you have a nearly unlimited choice of items to purchase. As an eBay seller you can sell almost any item with minimal setup costs.

HOW DID EBAY GET ITS NAME?

The founder of eBay, Pierre Omidyar, wanted to use the name "Echo Bay." As luck would have it, that name was already an incorporated business in California. On a whim, Pierre decided on eBay instead. The rest, as they say, is history.

HOW DOES EBAY WORK?

eBay works much like a standard auction house. The main differences are that the auction is controlled by the seller and it occurs over the Internet.

In a nutshell, here is how a typical eBay auction transpires:

1. A seller lists an item for sale on eBay.
2. Interested eBay members bid on the item.
3. At the end of the auction the bidder with the highest bid wins.
4. The buyer pays the seller.
5. The seller ships the item to the buyer.
6. Afterwards, both the buyer and seller leave feedback on each other's behavior during the transaction.

WHAT CAN I BUY ON EBAY?

You can buy virtually anything imaginable on eBay. Here's a short list of some of the item categories on eBay:

- House wares — dishes, curtains and kitchen appliances.
- Collectibles (dolls, coins, etc).
- Antiques and fine art.
- Computer hardware and software.
- Cars, boats and planes.
- Real Estate — time shares, vacation rentals or primary residences.
- Plants, seeds, and gardening supplies.
- Professional services.
- Toys and games.
- Tools and building supplies.
- Furniture.
- Consumer electronics.
- Clothes and costumes.
- Books and music.
- And many more categories are available.

IS EBAY FREE?

eBay does not charge anything for becoming a member, bidding in an auction or buying an item.

If you want to sell an item, then eBay charges you a small fee for listing the item and another small fee if the item sells.

WHO SELLS ITEMS ON EBAY?

All types of people and businesses sell items on eBay.

Most sellers are individuals like you and me. They may be downsizing their household or liquidating an antique collection. Generally, the items people list on eBay are in good-to-great shape, but they have no use for them.

Some people with a lot to sell opt to create an eBay Store. Either an individual, or an established company, can create an eBay Store. eBay Stores work just like other online merchants. Most stores list items at a fixed price as opposed to the bidding format of auctions. Although stores still have the option of conducting auctions.

Recently, large well-established companies started joining the eBay Community. For example, The Sharper Image and Sears each have an eBay presence.

WHAT CAN I SELL ON EBAY?

eBay will let you sell almost anything that anybody will buy. Just think of eBay as a giant flea market. If you put it up for sale someone may find value in it.

Before you start emptying your closets, be aware that your item needs to be in good shape. Old clothes and kid-seasoned toys generally don't do well on eBay. Buyers use eBay to find quality items, new or used, at reduced prices.

You should also consider how you plan to ship the items to the buyer before listing it on eBay. The harder it is to ship, the less likely you will find a buyer for it. For example, you might have problems selling your dining room table because of the shipping costs associated with it.

WHAT IS EBAY MOTORS?

eBay Motors is an online auction site dedicated to motor vehicles and accessories.

You can buy almost anything with an engine on eBay Motors: cars, trucks, motorcycles, boats, airplanes, snowmobiles and more. You can also find parts and accessories for modern and antique cars.

Bidding and selling on eBay Motors works like a typical eBay auction. However, paying is usually done in person when the winner picks up the vehicle. Often the winning bidder pays a deposit on the vehicle until he takes ownership.

So if you need a new car, motorcycle or anything else with an engine, give eBay Motors a spin!

WHAT ARE EBAY STORES?

eBay Stores offer regular sellers a more perma-
nent way to do business.

Sellers with a large inventory of various items
benefit the most from opening an eBay store
as it reduces the listing fees associated with
normal auctions.

Some other advantages an eBay Store offers
include the ability:

- To offer both fixed-priced or auction-
  based formats.
- To create up to eleven custom categories
  that are searchable.
- To promote your store from regular eBay
  auctions and the "About Me" page.

You can find a link to the eBay Stores from the
main eBay web page.

WHAT IS EBAY UNIVERSITY?

eBay wants you to learn as much as you can about buying, selling and using online auctions. As a result, eBay offers classes around the country by certified eBay instructors that can teach you all about eBay.

Class topics range from getting started to becoming a PowerSeller. You can find a class for any skill level or interest.

If you can't find a local class, you might consider taking one online. To find out more about eBay University, just check the Help page and click the <u>eBay University</u> link on the right-side of the page.

WHAT IS A TRADING ASSISTANT?

If you have items you want to sell, but are unsure how to do it or don't have the time, then consider using an eBay Trading Assistant.

Trading Assistants are very experienced eBay sellers who will sell your items for a fee. Trading Assistants typically perform the following services:

- Evaluate your item to determine if it has resale value.
- Research the market for your item.
- Write the item descriptions.
- Take digital photographs of the item.
- Collect money from the buyer.
- Ship the item to the buyer.

To locate a Trading Assistant in your area go to eBay's Services page and click the link <u>Trading Assistants</u> under the Advanced Seller Services section.

WHAT IS A TRADING POST?

Don't confuse a Trading Post with a Trading Assistant. Trading Posts are stores where you can drop off your item and they will sell it on eBay for you.

Trading Posts charge a small fee for selling your item. However, the store takes care of listing and shipping your item as well as collecting money from the buyer.

Trading Posts are manned by Trading Assistants. eBay has strict requirements for Trading Assistants that want to open a Trading Post. In particular, the eBay Web site states that a Trading Assistant must:

- Offer a staffed drop-off location or storefront with regular drop-in hours, so that clients can visit the location without calling ahead.
- Have a feedback score of 500 or higher.
- Have at least 98% positive feedback.
- Have sales of at least $25,000 on eBay each month.

Check your phone book or eBay to locate a Trading Post.

WHAT IS THE EBAY TOOLBAR?

eBay now has a Toolbar that plugs into Microsoft's Internet Explorer. eBay's Toolbar provides shortcuts to all the major eBay activities.

Here are few examples of what you can do with the eBay Toolbar:

- Check current bids.
- Go directly to the My eBay page.
- Review the items you have won.
- Access eBay's help system.
- Receive alerts on price changes.
- Search for items.

If you start using eBay a lot then you should consider using the Toolbar.

WHY SHOULD I USE EBAY?

eBay is a fantastic venue for buying and selling items from the comfort of your home.

If you have trouble going out to shop for Christmas or birthdays, eBay provides an electronic mall for you to find presents. You can also find items on eBay that you would like to have but don't want to purchase brand new.

Shopping on eBay is safe and secure. eBay keeps all of your financial and personal information locked away. Only you can see or change it. In addition, you can easily investigate who you are buying from or selling to. (We cover how to do this a little later in the book.) Thousands of transactions occur daily on eBay without incident.

WHY SHOULDN'T I USE EBAY?

eBay is not for everyone. The electronic and Internet-based environment may overwhelm some people.

Therefore, you may want to avoid eBay if you feel uncomfortable with emailing or paying electronically.

Also, if you need to see an item before buying it, then eBay obviously won't work for you. You very rarely get to personally look at something before buying it. The exceptions are large items such as boats and cars. Even then you need to travel to the seller so that you can see the vehicle.

You may also want to avoid eBay for high-end collectables unless the seller has stellar feedback and is a well-known dealer. You might find it difficult to properly authenticate and value antiques listed on eBay. Therefore it's probably best to stick with traditional auction houses for these types of items.

PART 2

Tools For Getting Started

With the introduction out of the way, let's go over the essential tools you need to start using eBay.

In this part we'll cover everything from computer requirements to payment methods. After reading this Part you should be ready to become an eBay member.

WHAT DO I NEED TO GET STARTED?

Getting started on eBay is simple. However, you do need access to the following:

- A computer.
- An Internet connection.
- An email address.
- A way to pay for items that you purchase.
- A way to collect payment for items that you sell.

WHAT TYPE OF COMPUTER DO I NEED?

You need a moderately-powered computer to fully enjoy eBay. That said, enjoyment is relative. If your computer is fast enough for you to enjoy the Internet, then it's likely fast enough to enjoy eBay.

The computer type you use is irrelevant. eBay works with both Macs and PCs. eBay also works with most web browsers. However you should probably stick with Internet Explorer or Netscape Navigator to ensure compatibility.

Because eBay is Internet-based, you do not need any special software to use it. There are no installation diskettes or cd-roms. All you need to do is open http://www.eBay.com in your web browser.

You can still use eBay if you do not have a computer. Just use a computer at your local library, a friend's house, your children's house or senior center. Do not forget, eBay is Internet-based, which means you can access it from virtually anywhere using almost any type of computer.

WHAT TYPE OF INTERNET CONNECTION DO I NEED?

More important than the type of computer is the type of Internet connection you have. The rule of thumb here is the faster the connection, the better.

A slow connection, such as a 56k dial-up, can give you an unpleasant eBay experience. You will spend a lot of time waiting for images to load instead of shopping.

Ideally, you should use a broadband Internet connection such as a cable modem, satellite or DSL. This will allow the eBay web pages to load quickly. If you want to sell, then a fast Internet connection will also let you quickly upload your auction pictures.

If you don't have a broadband connection, contact your local cable, satellite or phone company for more information.

However, you can still connect with eBay on a standard dial-up connection.

WHAT TYPE OF EMAIL ACCOUNT DO I NEED?

Any email account will do. Just remember, you MUST have an email account to use eBay. Email is the primary communication means between you, eBay and other eBay members.

If you do not have an email address, consider signing up for a free email account with Hotmail, Yahoo!, Google or other email provider. Your Internet Service Provider may also provide you with an email address you can use.

Once you start using eBay, your email account becomes your lifeline to the eBay Community. Check your email frequently once you start becoming active on eBay.

HOW DO I PAY FOR ITEMS?

If you buy an item on eBay the seller has the final word on how you must pay for an item. In other words, sellers set the payment method.

However, sellers want to collect their money so they often accept a variety of payment methods. Most sellers accept money orders, electronic checks, credit cards, bank transfers and PayPal.

The most popular, and highly recommended, payment method on eBay is PayPal. eBay owns PayPal so the service is tightly integrated within the auction checkout system. eBay's Checkout Feature is a perfect example of a well integrated payment system.

You should consider opening a PayPal account to make buying and selling items on eBay easier.

WHAT IS PAYPAL?

PayPal is an electronic transaction processing service owned by eBay. Before PayPal, sellers had to set up a special merchant account with a financial institution like a bank, to accept credit cards. Now, a PayPal account allows sellers to accept a wide variety of credit cards with minimal setup fees or hassles.

PayPal also has benefits for the buyer as well. Paying with a credit card via PayPal is very secure and very fast. As a buyer you do not have to worry about the safety of the online transactions and as a seller you receive your payment almost immediately. The fast turnaround can result in you receiving your item quicker.

Remember, since eBay owns PayPal, the service is integrated into eBay's auction system.

PayPal can be used for non-eBay transactions as well. Numerous other online stores and ecommerce sites accept PayPal. It is the standard for online transaction processing.

Go to http://www.PayPal.com for more information on opening an account. We also provide some basic instructions for opening a PayPal account in Part 3.

Joining The eBay Community

In this Part we walk you through the process of joining the eBay Community.

Once you read this part you will know how to become an eBay member and navigate eBay's web site. We cover topics such as finding eBay on the Internet, choosing a User ID, submitting and verifying your membership application, and understanding eBay's Feedback system.

HOW DO I FIND EBAY ON THE INTERNET?

To find the eBay web site:

1. Open your web browser (Internet Explorer or Netscape Navigator).
2. Type http://www.ebay.com in the Address box.
3. Press Enter on your keyboard.

Your browser should open up the eBay home page. At the top of the page you will find the eBay Menu, which has all the links you need to navigate the eBay site.

WHAT IS THE EBAY MENU?

The eBay Menu, shown in Figure 1, appears on almost every eBay web page.

From eBay's menu you can:

• Start browsing for items.
• Search for a specific item.
• Register for an eBay account.
• Open the online help pages.
• Sell something.
• Sign-in to your eBay account.

We will cover each of these activities later in the book. For now, just remember the eBay Menu helps you get to where you want to go.

home | pay | register | sign in | services | site map

| Buy | Sell | My eBay | Community | Help |

Figure 1: eBay Menu

WHAT IS THE SERVICES LINK?

Clicking the <u>Services</u> link opens a web page that lists all of eBay's services. Think of it as an index of eBay's services.

On the Services page you can find information about:

- Seller's tools such as promotional programs, warranty plans, and listing solutions.
- Buyer's programs such as buyer protection and the Feedback Forum.
- Payment services such as PayPal and financing options.
- Advanced seller programs such as eBay Stores and the PowerSeller program.
- Links to eBay's customer service center.

This list provides only a sample of the information on the eBay Services web page. Whenever you have a question, open the Services page for answers (or you can send your question to us at <u>www.theseniorsguide.com</u>).

HOW DO I OPEN AN EBAY ACCOUNT?

Becoming an eBay member is simple, just click on the <u>register</u> link on the eBay Menu.

Figure 2 below identifies the <u>register</u> link for you.

Click <u>register</u> to become
an eBay member.

home | pay | register | sign in | services | site map

Buy	Sell	My eBay	Community	Help

Figure 2: eBay Menu — register link.

WHAT ARE THE EBAY
REGISTRATION STEPS?

The eBay registration process has the
following steps:

1. Provide personal information such as name,
   address, phone number and email address.
2. Choose an eBay User ID and password.
3. Agree to the eBay User Agreement and
   Privacy Policy.
4. Receive a confirmation email and follow the
   instructions for confirming your registration.

WHAT SHOULD I KNOW
BEFORE I REGISTER?

Although eBay registration is simple, there are two points you should remember.

First, you need to understand that your registration is not complete unless you respond to the confirmation email. When you respond to the email, eBay knows that the email address works and that you are sincere about becoming an eBay member.

NOTE: If you do not confirm your registration, eBay will ignore your application.

Secondly, eBay will request a credit card to verify your identity if you use a free email service such as Hotmail or Yahoo!.

Why? Most free email services do not verify your identity when you signup. eBay checks your credit card to make sure you are who you say you are. At no time is your credit card charged anything!

eBay verifies your identity to protect the eBay Community. Knowing who people are has helped create eBay's safe shopping environment.

WHAT SHOULD I KNOW ABOUT CHOOSING A USER ID?

You might find that choosing a User ID is difficult. After all, choosing a User ID is like naming yourself!

Here are a couple of suggestions for choosing a User ID:

- Consider choosing a User ID that is short and easy to remember. Using your initials and a number make an easy User ID. For instance: tmt1213 is short and simple.
- Choose a User ID that reflects your interest as a buyer or seller. For example if you like flowers you could choose the User ID "flowershopper."

WHAT SHOULD I KNOW ABOUT
CHOOSING A PASSWORD?

The password you choose is very important. Try to choose something that is easy to remember but hard for others to figure out. Consider the following guidelines when choosing an eBay password:

- Passwords must be at least six characters long.
- Never user your eBay User ID as your password.
- Never use your name or names of a family member as a password.
- Try to use both letters and numbers in the password (e.g. pa55w0rd).

HOW DO I CONFIRM MY REGISTRATION?

eBay sends you a confirmation email once you submit your member registration.

The confirmation email contains a button to click that takes you to the eBay registration confirmation page. Clicking the button also sends the information needed by eBay to complete the registration process.

Depending upon your email client, the confirmation button may not appear in the email. In this case, click the <u>site map</u> link on the eBay Menu, then click the <u>Confirm Registration</u> link under Services section. This will allow you to manually confirm your registration. Note that you need the registration number contained in your email to complete the process.

Remember, you must confirm your registration or eBay will ignore your membership request.

HOW DO I TROUBLESHOOT
REGISTRATION PROBLEMS?

Sometimes, but not very often, the eBay registration process does hiccup. Problems arise mainly from errors in the information a prospective member provides.

The biggest single issue that occurs is an invalid email address was submitted. If you don't receive a confirmation email soon after you register, you probably should go back and check that your email address is correct.

Another problem that regularly occurs is if an invalid credit card number is entered during the verification process. If this happens, just reenter the correct number to correct the problem.

If you have other problems, email eBay's help desk and they will promptly assist you. Click the Help link on the eBay toolbar, then the Becoming a Member link.

Don't worry; eBay will be glad to help you. After all, they want you to buy and sell on eBay!

HOW DO I OPEN A PAYPAL ACCOUNT?

A PayPal account is optional. You do not need one to use eBay. However, because most sellers accept PayPal as a payment method and it very safe, you should go ahead and create an account. If you don't use it now, you might in the future. Besides, like eBay, PayPal accounts are free!

To sign up:

1. Navigate to www.paypal.com.
2. Click the Sign Up link.
3. Choose a personal account then choose your country of residence. Click the **Continue** button.
4. Fill out the Account Sign Up form, which consists of entering your name, address and some security information.
5. Wait for PayPal to send you a confirmation email.
6. Once your email arrives, follow the instructions to verify your account. You will need the password you entered on the Account Sign Up form to complete this process.

HOW DO I OPEN A PAYPAL ACCOUNT?, CONT.

Now you have a PayPal account. Before it becomes fully functional you must enable a payment method. You can choose to add a credit card or bank account. To add an account, click the Add credit card or Add bank account link to complete this process.

HOW DO I CHANGE MY PERSONAL INFORMATION?

From time to time you may need to change your eBay personal information. For instance, if you move or get a different email address, you will need to change it in your eBay profile. You can change almost any piece of personal information you have; your User ID, password, email address, shipping address, etc.

To make changes just follow these steps:

1. Click the <u>My eBay</u> link on the eBay Menu to access your account information.
2. If necessary, enter your User ID and password.
3. Next click the <u>Personal Information</u> link on the right side of the page, which loads a page where you can change your information.
4. Click the <u>change</u> link beside the information you wish to change.
5. You must re-enter your password for security reasons.
6. Follow the instructions for changing the specific information.

WHAT IF I FORGET MY USER ID?

If you only use eBay periodically, you may forget your User ID. Don't worry, hundreds of people forget theirs everyday. eBay empathizes and will email it to you.

Follow these steps to request your User ID:

1. Click the <u>sign in</u> link on the eBay Menu.
2. Click the <u>Forgot</u> link under the text box where you normally enter your User ID.
3. Enter the email address you gave eBay when signing up for the account.
4. Wait until eBay sends you an email with your User ID. It could take several hours for the email to arrive.

WHAT IF I FORGET MY PASSWORD?

More than likely you will remember your User ID but forget your password. Once again, don't worry, eBay allows you to reset your password. However, you need to provide some extra information to verify your identity before you can reset your password. eBay takes this extra step to help protect your account. Once eBay confirms who you are they will email instructions on how to reset your password.

To recover your password:

1. Click the <u>sign in</u> link on the eBay Menu.
2. Click the <u>Forgot</u> link under the text box where you normally enter your password.
3. On the next page enter your eBay User ID then click the **Continue** button.
4. Answer one of several questions presented to verify your identity.
5. Wait until eBay sends you an email with a link to an eBay page.
6. Click the link in the email that eBay sends you.
7. Enter your User ID and click the **Continue** button.
8. Choose a new password and click the **Change Password** button.

WHAT IS THE USER AGREEMENT?

The User Agreement is a contract between you and eBay stating what you, other members and eBay can and cannot do.

You should read it carefully so you know the rules that all registered members must follow.

WHAT IS EBAY'S PRIVACY POLICY?

eBay's Privacy Policy states how eBay will use the personal information that you provided when you became a member.

In a nutshell, the policy states that eBay will not share any information with third party advertisers like email spammers or direct mail services. However, eBay may use the information internally to help improve the services that you use most.

WHAT IS THE EBAY COMMUNITY?

The eBay Community is a virtual "club" consisting of eBay members. Clicking the <u>Community</u> link on the eBay Menu will take you to the Community web page.

eBay members join the Community to gather and share stories, learn about eBay, and discuss common interests. You can even subscribe to a monthly email newsletter to keep up with eBay events.

The eBay Community is quite large and diverse. It has areas dedicated to:

- News such as eBay announcements and system status.
- eBay members, which includes special interest groups and member spotlights.
- Special events such as workshops and web seminars.
- Discussion boards and chat rooms to share similar interests and offer assistance.

Participating in the community is a great way to learn about eBay and help others learn about eBay.

WHAT ARE THE EBAY COMMUNITY VALUES?

eBay takes its community seriously. Without the community, eBay would not work as well as it does.

To show their commitment to honesty and integrity, eBay has adopted five Community Values that members should follow.

From the eBay web site, the five Community Values are:

- We believe people are basically good.
- We believe everyone has something to contribute.
- We believe that an honest, open environment can bring out the best in people.
- We recognize and respect everyone as a unique individual.
- We encourage you to treat others the way that you want to be treated.

WHAT IS THE EBAY SITE MAP?

The site map provides an index to eBay's vast web site. It can help you quickly find links to the information you need on the entire site. Make a habit of using it. It will save you time in the long run.

Figure 3 below identifies the eBay site map link for you.

Click site map to open
eBay's Web site index.

home | pay | register | sign in | services | site map

Buy	Sell	My eBay	Community	Help

Figure 3: eBay Menu — site map link.

WHAT IS EBAY FEEDBACK?

eBay, above all else, is based on trust. A seller trusts that the buyer will pay for an item, while a buyer trusts that the seller will ship the item. eBay creates this trusting environment using Feedback.

eBay members drive the Feedback system by rating each other after a transaction. If the exchange was satisfactory, the buyer, or seller, receives positive feedback. Likewise, if the transaction was unsatisfactory, the buyer or seller receives negative feedback.

Also, because eBay promotes openness and honesty, you can easily find out how other members behave by reviewing their feedback. The eBay Feedback system allows you to look at your trading partner's reputation. As equally important, your trading partners can see your reputation.

Why is feedback beneficial? As a buyer you want to determine if the seller is legitimate. As a seller you want to determine if the buyer will pay for your item. Reviewing feedback can help ensure a safe transaction for both parties.

Remember, eBay doesn't participate in the Feedback, members do.

WHAT IS THE FEEDBACK FORUM?

The Feedback Forum is part of eBay's Feedback system.

eBay members go to the Feedback Forum and leave public comments about other eBay members. So if a buyer didn't receive an item in the expected condition, they can go to the Forum and post negative feedback about the seller.

Likewise, if a buyer didn't follow through with a transaction, then a seller could post negative feedback about the buyer.

As an eBay member you can also go to the Feedback Forum to view feedback on other members. All you need to know is the User ID and you can check out their past behavior.

HOW DO I REVIEW A
MEMBER'S FEEDBACK?

To find another member's Feedback just go to the Feedback Forum. Follow these directions to review another member's feedback:

1. Click the <u>services</u> link on the eBay Menu.
2. Click the <u>eBay Feedback Forum</u> link in the Member Reputation section.
3. Once in the Forum, enter the member's User ID and click the **Find Member** button.

WHAT IS POSITIVE, NEGATIVE, AND NEUTRAL FEEDBACK?

Members are rated using three categories of feedback. The following list describes the three different types of feedback:

- **Positive** — means the transaction went well and you are satisfied. Positive feedback is worth one (1) point in eBay's Feedback Rating system.
- **Neutral** — means that the transaction was okay, but nothing stellar. *Neutral feedback* is worth zero (0) points in eBay's Feedback system.
- **Negative** — means the transaction was not satisfactory. Buyers can receive negative feedback if they don't pay on time or at all. Sellers receive negative feedback for misleading the buyer. Negative feedback is worth negative one (-1) point in eBay's Feedback Rating system.

If a member does not have any feedback then they will have a feedback score of zero.

WHAT ARE EBAY STARS?

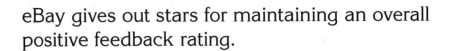

eBay gives out stars for maintaining an overall positive feedback rating.

Remember, points are awarded for the type of feedback you receive: one (1) point for positive, zero (0) points for neutral, and minus one (-1) point for negative. All the points from your feedback are added together to get your overall score.

Stars are given for the following Feedback scores:

- Gold — 10 to 49 points.
- Blue — 50 to 99 points.
- Turquoise — 100 to 499 points.
- Red — 1,000 to 4,999 points.
- Green — 5,000 to 9,999 points.
- Shooting Yellow — 10,000 to 24,999 points.
- Shooting Turquoise — 25,000 to 49,999 points.
- Shooting Purple — 50,000 to 99,999 points.
- Shooting Red — 100,000 points or higher.

Most of the time a higher feedback rating is good. However, be sure to review the member's feedback for details on their most recent behavior.

HOW DO I EARN A GOOD REPUTATION?

Earning and keeping a good reputation in the eBay Community is essential to being a successful eBay seller or buyer.

Here are some hints to help you maintain a glowing reputation:

- Respond to emails quickly.
- Pay as soon as possible when you buy something.
- Ship the item as soon as you receive payment.
- Keep your word.

WHAT IS MY EBAY?

When you become an eBay member you get a My eBay web page. This page is the control center for all of your eBay activity.

To find your My eBay page, simply click the My eBay link on the eBay Menu. If you haven't signed in, then you need to provide your User ID and password.

On the My eBay page you will find:

- Your current buying and selling activities.
- Favorite searches, sellers and eBay Stores.
- Auctions you are currently watching.
- Email notification settings for items you are watching.
- Auctions you have won, lost, or currently bidding on.

As you can see, the My eBay page provides you with a lot of information. You should refer to it often.

WHAT IS ABOUT ME?

eBay provides you with a homepage when you become a member. You can use the homepage to tell more about yourself and what you like to buy or sell.

Most people do not bother to setup an About Me homepage. However, you should take advantage of the About Me page to promote your auctions or eBay store if you are a seller.

You can access your About Me page using the services link on the eBay Menu. Just follow the instructions and you can have you own eBay homepage in no time.

IS EBAY A TYPE OF E-COMMERCE?

Yes. Now that you are part of the eBay Community, you are ready to experience e-commerce. Like any other business, there is a certain learning curve associated with operating the eBay system. Don't worry if it takes you a few times to get comfortable with the process.

PART 4

Searching And Browsing For Bargains

In this Part we present how to find items on eBay.

We start by discussing how to search for specific items such as blenders or antique clocks. With eBay's search tools you can quickly locate the exact item you want to buy.

We also discuss how to browse, or window shop for an item. You might browse for an item when looking for a gift or a birthday present.

SHOULD I BROWSE OR SEARCH?

Whether you browse or search depends on what you want to do.

As an example, let's assume you want to buy a digital camera. If you know exactly which camera you want, such as a Nikon CoolPix 8700, then a search will list all the items related to that model.

However, searching will not only list that specific camera for sale, but also accessories such as lens covers and camera bags that go with the Nikon 8700. If you only want camera listings, then you must plow through the results or refine your search. We discuss how to refine your search a little later.

You should browse if you want to window shop for cameras. Browsing allows you to peruse eBay's item categories. So when looking for a digital camera you could browse the different camera categories such as Point-and-Shoot, Professional, Low Resolution, etc. Browsing can let you find an item that matches your buying criteria regardless of brand.

HOW DO I START SEARCHING
OR BROWSING?

Figure 4 below shows you the links to click to start Searching or Browsing.

Click <u>Buy</u> to search for
items on eBay.

<u>home</u> | <u>pay</u> | <u>register</u> | <u>sign in</u> | <u>services</u> | <u>site map</u>

Buy	Sell	My eBay	Community	Help

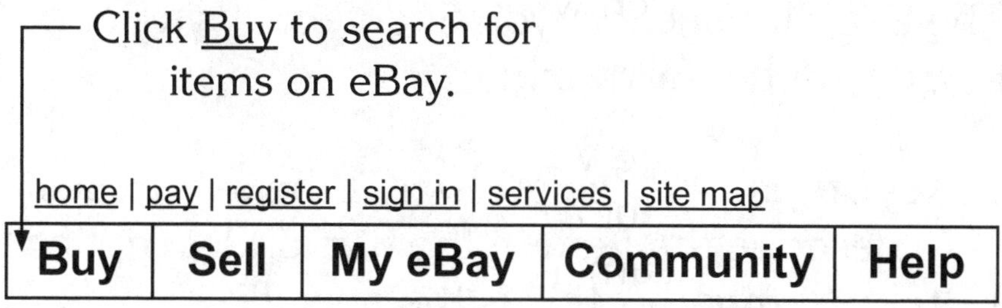

Figure 4: eBay Menu — Search
and Browse Links

HOW DO I SEARCH FOR AN ITEM?

With millions of items for sale on eBay you may think it would be hard to find the item you want. But not so! Searching on eBay is easy. Just click the <u>Search</u> link on the eBay Menu to load the Search page.

The Search page lets you find items using one or more of the following:

- **Keywords** — these are words the seller uses to describe the item in the title or description.
- **Item Number** — this is the specific eBay item number for an item. It is unique, just like your Social Security Number.
- **Category** — allows you to search for items in a specific category. If you do not specify an item description, keyword, or item number, then all items in a category are listed.

Most members search for items using keywords. For example, you might use "photography digital camera" as keywords when searching for a digital camera.

HOW DO I SEARCH FOR AN ITEM?, CONT.

To perform a search, just type in the keywords and either press Enter on your keyboard or click on the **Search** button located on the eBay Search page.

One thing to remember is that a search, by default, only looks at an item's title and not its description. You can search the description as well by clicking the check box underneath the search phrase.

WHAT ARE SOME SEARCHING HINTS?

Searching eBay can seem confusing at times. Often you get more listings than expected, most of which are irrelevant with respect to the specific item you are looking for.

Below are a few hints you can use to improve your searching:

- eBay keywords are not case specific.
- Search in both the titles and item descriptions to return more items.
- Try removing the "s" from plural keywords such as "cups" to expand the number of items returned.
- Use the exact name, model number or brand of an item.
- Use specific words instead of general, ex: baseball instead of sports.
- Use punctuation only when needed.
- Avoid using "and", "or", "the."

HOW DO I REFINE MY SEARCHES?

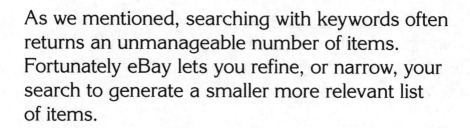

As we mentioned, searching with keywords often returns an unmanageable number of items. Fortunately eBay lets you refine, or narrow, your search to generate a smaller more relevant list of items.

eBay has several methods to refine a search. The easiest way is to combine keywords and eBay categories. For example, when looking for oil paintings, you may want to search only in the "Art" category, which will confine your search to that area.

Another way to refine a search is to use eBay's search options. These are user-friendly options you can use to fine tune your search.

The final method is to use Advanced Search techniques. This method is a little cryptic, but very powerful. Briefly, it uses special symbols, such as "+", in unison with keywords to refine your search.

Choosing the best way to narrow your search depends upon the item. For example, some items have a lot of accessories and to pare down your search you will need to exclude certain words.

WHAT ARE EBAY'S SEARCH OPTIONS?

Click <u>More search options</u> link on the Search page to reveal additional ways to search for an item. The following list provides an overview of the additional search options:

- **Exclude these words** — do not display items with certain words in the title or item description.
- **Items Priced** — specify a minimum and/or maximum price range for the item.
- **From specific sellers** — show only items from specific sellers.
- **Location** — narrow the items displayed to a certain country.

You can use any of these options alone, or in combination.

The best way to learn how to use the options is to play around with them. Pick an item and change the options to produce different results. eBay doesn't charge for searching, so practice as much as you want.

WHAT IS AN ADVANCED SEARCH?

An advanced search allows you to use special search characters, such as the "*" and "+" symbols, along with keywords to further refine your search.

You can also use Advanced Searches with the other search criteria listed on the eBay Search page. The advance search symbols provide a powerful toolset to help you find the exact item you want.

In the next few pages we provide examples on how to create and perform advanced searches.

WHAT DOES THE ADVANCED SEARCH "*" DO?

The asterisk, "*", appended to the end of a word will return all items that start with that word.

Example

Search Phrase: foot*

Results: Returns items such as football, footstool, footpad, footwear, etc. in the title.

WHAT DOES THE ADVANCED SEARCH " " DO?

You can use quotations marks, " ", to specify the exact order of keywords you want to appear in the title or descriptions.

Example

Search Phrase: "glass hummingbird feeder"

Results: Returns items with the exact phrase, glass hummingbird feeder, in the title.

WHAT DOES THE ADVANCED SEARCH "-" DO?

As you might expect, the minus, "-", symbol excludes keywords from searches. This symbol will help refine your search by excluding words or phrases in the item's title.

Example

Search Phrase: football –autograph

Results: Returns all items with the word football in the title but excludes items with both football and autograph.

Note: Do not place a space after the "-" symbol.

WHAT DOES THE ADVANCED SEARCH "()" DO?

The parenthesis, "()", allows you to search for one keyword or another. In essence, the parenthesis performs an "or" search by looking for any keyword in the title. You may use as many keywords within the parenthesis as you want.

Example

Search Phrase: (Nikon,Canon,Olympus).

Results: Returns all items with the words Nikon OR Canon OR Olympus in the title.

Note: Do not put a space between the keywords.

WHAT DOES THE ADVANCED SEARCH "+" DO?

The plus symbol, "+", before a word indicates that it is required. You can use this symbol to make some advance searches more flexible.

Example

Search phrase: (football,baseball) +tickets.

Results: Returns items with football or baseball along with ticket in the title.

Note: Do not put a space after the "+" symbol.

WHAT ARE FAVORITE SEARCHES?

Favorite Searches are searches you save so you can easily search for the item again. This is helpful for searches in which you spend time refining your search using search categories and special symbols. Saving it keeps you from having to reenter the search criteria again.

You might consider creating a Favorite Search for an item you search for regularly. Creating Favorite Searches is an excellent way to save time and replicate a complex search.

Access the Favorite Searches from the eBay Search page or your "My eBay" page.

HOW DO I CREATE A FAVORITE SEARCH?

To set up a Favorite Search, follow these steps:

1. Search for an item as normal. Be sure to refine the search to display the exact items you want.
2. Once the listing is displayed click the <u>Favorite Search</u> link in the upper right corner.
3. Follow the instructions to save the search.
4. The next time you want to look for the item go to your "My eBay" page and click on the item under "Favorite Searches."

HOW DO I SEARCH WHILE I'M SLEEPING?

Looking for that special item at the right price, condition or location, but have limited time to do so? Don't despair, let eBay look for you and then send an email when a new item appears that matches your criteria.

For example, suppose you want to buy a china cabinet for less than $500, and it must be located near Orlando. Instead of performing an advanced search everyday, do the search once and save it as a Favorite Search.

Once you saved the search, you can turn on the email notification from the "My eBay" page. This option is located beside the Favorite Search title. Now when an item appears, eBay will send you an email. Just click the link in the email to view the item on eBay.

Of course you will have to check you email frequently to make sure you do not miss a good deal!

HOW DO I BROWSE FOR AN ITEM?

As mentioned earlier, you may want to browse if you aren't sure what you are looking for or just want to window shop eBay's vast variety of items.

To start browsing, just click on the <u>Browse</u> link on the eBay Menu. The Browsing page lists all of eBay's categories. Click on the category of interest to display its sub-categories. Continue in this manner until you find what you want.

You can also start Browsing from the eBay home page; just click a category to begin.

WHAT ARE HOT ITEMS?

A hot item is one in which a lot of buyers place
a lot bids in short time.

To qualify as a hot item, the item must receive
more than thirty bids and not have a reserve
price. Hot items generally sell at premium prices.

When an item meets those criteria, eBay places
a "match" icon next to the item. You will see
the icon in both the search result listings and
browsing lists.

WHAT ARE HIDDEN GEMS?

Hidden gems are items in which the seller has made a mistake in the listing process. The seller may have placed the item in the wrong category or misspelled a word in the description.

As a result of the mistake, you can often buy these items at bargain prices because no one else can find them.

For example, searching for "kup" instead of "cup" may yield some interesting items. Some of them may be under priced hidden gems. Searching for hidden gems can be fun, and may be profitable.

PART 5

Understanding eBay Auctions

In this Part we explain how eBay auctions work. We cover topics on shopping safety, determining how much time is left in an auction and reading the item description.

After you read this Part you will be prepared to place bids in an auction.

WHAT DO I NEED TO BUY ITEMS ON EBAY?

To participate on eBay you need a member account, email address and a way to pay for your items.

Obviously it makes sense that to shop on eBay you must be a member. Follow the advice in Part 2 — Becoming An eBay Member for more information on how to join the eBay Community.

You also need an email address you can check regularly. You should check your email in the morning and evening when you start communicating with buyers and sellers.

If you are using a computer not in your own home, make sure you know the times you have access to it. Timely communication helps you earn positive feedback.

The seller dictates the payment method for an item. Some take credit cards directly, e-checks, or money orders while others only accept PayPal.

Even if you don't plan to do a lot of eBay shopping you should open a PayPal account. We provide an overview of how to open a PayPal account in Part 3.

HOW DOES AN EBAY AUCTION WORK?

An eBay auction works similarly to a traditional live auction, except it occurs online. Here are the basic steps in an eBay auction:

1. A seller creates an auction for an item he/she wishes to sell.
2. Interested buyers place bids on that item.
3. Buyers periodically check the bids and place a higher bid if they want the item.
4. At the end of the auction the bidder with the highest bid wins the item.
5. The winner pays the seller, who in turn ships the item to the sender.
6. After the auction the buyer and seller leave feedback about each other.

ARE ONLINE EBAY PAYMENTS SAFE?

Yes, online payments on eBay are safe, especially if you use PayPal.

As we mentioned earlier, eBay owns the PayPal electronic payment service. As you might imagine eBay's payment system centers on PayPal.

You can be assured that if you buy items using PayPal, your money and your account are well protected.

You should exercise caution if you pay the seller using other electronic methods besides the eBay payment service.

It also is worth learning more about buyer protection programs like PayPal's Buyer Protection and eBay's Standard Protection Program. We cover these programs in Part 7.

HOW CAN I SHOP SAFELY ON EBAY?

Ultimately, safe shopping is your personal responsibility. However, you should not have any problems if you thoroughly research the seller and the item.

Here are three rules you should follow to help ensure a safe transaction:

- **Rule 1** — Review the seller's Feedback to understand their history and experience.
- **Rule 2** — Read the item description carefully to understand its condition, shipping information, payment methods, and if the seller has a return policy.
- **Rule 3** — Ask the seller questions during the auction if you have any doubts or concerns about any charge or item condition.

From the above rules, reviewing the seller's feedback and reading the item description are the two most important rules you can follow to ensure a safe transaction. Don't assume sellers are honest just because they have auction listings.

WHAT IS THE SELLER INFORMATION BOX?

You will find the Seller Information box on every eBay auction. It contains valuable information about the seller such as the feedback score and links to contact the seller.

Figure 5 below provides an example of the Seller Information box.

Figure 5: Seller Information Box

HOW DO I LEARN ABOUT A SELLER?

Remember, the first rule in safe shopping is to review the seller's Feedback. eBay provides the Feedback Forum for this very purpose.

The easiest way to view a seller's feedback is to click the seller's User ID in the Seller Information box on the item's auction page. This page lists the feedback about a seller. You can quickly see how reputable the seller is by reviewing the feedback.

You can also learn about the member who left the feedback, by clicking on their User ID. This is a good idea, especially if a member left negative feedback about the seller.

The dissatisfied member could be a habitual complainer, in which case you could discount their feedback.

HOW MUCH SHOULD I LEARN
ABOUT THE SELLER?

The short answer is as much as possible. However, you can only learn so much in eBay's Feedback Forum.

At a minimum you want to know about the seller's experience and reputation.

Here is a list of some important things to learn about the seller:

- How long has the seller been a member of e-Bay?
- How many auctions does the seller currently have?
- How many auctions has the seller conducted?
- Does the seller have negative feedback?
- Is the seller a PowerSeller?
- Does the seller accept returns?

The ideal seller should have a lot of experience and a glowing reputation.

WHY SHOULD I READ THE ITEM DESCRIPTION?

The second rule of safe shopping is that you should always read, and understand, the item description. It contains essential information about the auction.

In particular, the seller places details about the item, payment methods, and his return policy in the description. Always, without fail, read the item description!

The item description may answer important questions such as:

- Why the seller is auctioning the item?
- What is the condition of the item?
- How old is the item?
- Is the item new or used?
- What is the seller's return policy?
- What payment method does the seller accept?

Along with the seller's feedback and profile, the item description can help you decide if you trust the seller and want to buy the product. If you read the description and still have questions, do not hesitate to contact the seller.

HOW DO I ASK THE SELLER A QUESTION?

The third rule of safe shopping is to ask the seller any question you have about the item for sale. Besides answering your question, it might prompt him/her to add an important piece of information to the item description page.

To ask a question, click the <u>Ask seller question</u> link located in the Seller Information box on the Item description page.

When asking a question, try to make it as detailed as possible to help the seller provide you with accurate information.

WHAT IF A SELLER HAS NEGATIVE FEEDBACK?

Don't write off a seller just because of negative feedback. Some sellers may have negative feedback, just as some businesses may have unhappy customers. The saying "You can't please everyone", certainly applies to eBay as well.

You should consider several factors before making a decision about a seller with negative feedback.

First, did a "grumpy" member leave the feedback? That is, has the member also left negative feedback about other sellers? If so, that buyer could be a habitual complainer, so you might discount his/her opinion.

Secondly, consider how long ago the negative feedback occurred. More recent negative feedback should carry more weight. If it was a long time ago, it may have occurred as the seller was learning about the eBay selling process.

Lastly, what's the nature of the feedback? A complaint about a poorly described item is different from a complaint about an item that arrived late, broken, or not at all.

Judging negative feedback is not straight-forward. However, you can always contact the seller to get more information on their feedback and the product. Don't hesitate to ask!

WHAT IS A POWERSELLER?

A PowerSeller is a designation given to sellers who consistently meet a certain sales volume and provide outstanding customer service.

To qualify for PowerSeller status a seller must receive at least 98% positive feedback from buyers. The sales volume depends upon the items in which the seller auctions.

You probably can feel comfortable buying from a PowerSeller. However, you should still carefully read the item's description and seller's profile before buying.

HOW DO I WATCH AN ITEM?

When you find an item you want to buy, try "watching" it to see how the bidding progresses.

To watch an item, just click the <u>Watch Item</u> link in the upper-right corner on the item description page. Doing so places a link to the item on your "My eBay" page. Clicking the link will load the auction page, which saves you from having to search for the item again.

eBay will also send you email reminders about when the auction will end for watched items.

WHERE CAN I FIND BID INFORMATION FOR AN ITEM?

At the top of an auction page you will find the Bid Information section. This section contains all you need to evaluate the bidding activity for an item. You can find the current bid, time remaining in the auction, the highest bidder, and much more. Figure 6 below shows an example of the Bid Information section.

Current bid:	**US $760.00**
	Place Bid>
Time left:	**4 hours 25 mins** 3-day listing Ends Nov-03-04 16:05:52 PST
Start time:	Oct-31-04 16:05:52 PST
History:	23 bids (US $100.00 starting bid)
High bidder:	sellername (14 ☆)
Item location:	Irvington, New Jersey United States
Featured Plus! Listing	
Ships to:	Americas
Shipping costs:	Check item description and payment instructions or contact seller for details

Figure 6: Bid Information

WHAT IS THE STARTING BID?

The starting bid of an auction is the minimum price of the item. This is the price at which the seller wants the bidding to begin. You will only see the starting bid listed if no other bids have been placed. If bids exist, the current bid will be listed instead.

For items with a reserve you might see a ridiculously low starting bid. The seller sets the starting bid very low to stimulate bidding and to reduce the initial listing fees. Don't think you will win a DVD player for $0.99!

WHAT IS THE CURRENT BID?

The current bid is the highest bid another eBay member has placed on the item. When the auction ends, the current bid wins because it is also the highest bid.

When you look at an item's auction page, the current bid is the first line in the Bid Information section. If you want to bid on this item, you must place a bid greater than the current bid. We cover bidding in more detail in Part 6.

WHAT IS A RESERVE PRICE?

The reserve price is the minimum price a seller will take for an item. Unfortunately, as a bidder you cannot see the reserve price.

You can tell the seller set a reserve price if the phrase "Reserve Not Yet Met" or "Reserve Met" appears beside the item's current bid.

If the current bid is below the reserve price then the phrase "Reserve Not Yet Met" is displayed. Once the current bid equals or exceeds the seller's reserve price, then the phrase "Reserve Met" appears.

Sellers have the right not to sell the item if the current bid is below the reserve price at the end of the auction. However, you can always approach the seller via email after the auction to see if you can negotiate a fair price. It never hurts to ask!

WHAT ARE THE ADDITIONAL COSTS OF BUYING?

You should read the item description and the Shipping and Payment sections carefully before placing a bid. You may find hidden costs for an item that you think is a bargain.

Here are few examples of the hidden costs:

- **Shipping** — check to see if the item has a fixed or variable shipping rate. If the item is large, or requires special shipping, then the rate may vary.
- **Handling** — some sellers charge a legitimate handling fee to cover the labor and materials required to send the item.
- **Taxes** — if you buy an item locally, or within your State, you may be liable for sales tax.
- **Shipping insurance** — if you want shipping insurance to protect the item, then you will need to add this cost to your maximum bid.

Once again, if you have any questions about the charges, ask the seller via email.

WHAT IS THE TOTAL NUMBER OF BIDS?

The total number of bids indicates the interest level for an item. An item with a lot of interest has a lot of bids. Auctions with a lot of activity generally bring a premium price.

You can determine the number of bids (e.g. 3 bids) by looking at the "History" section shown on an item's auction page. Clicking the number of bids provides more details on the bid history.

WHAT IS THE BUY IT NOW OPTION?

The "Buy It Now" option provides a way for you to purchase an item without bidding on it. It is the price the buyer will sell the item to you this instant.

When you buy an item via "Buy It Now", you do not have to wait until the auction ends. You can purchase it immediately without placing a bid.

Sellers may use a "Buy It Now" listing to move an item fast by giving bidders an opportunity to purchase the item immediately.

WHAT IS THE EBAY OFFICIAL TIME?

eBay is located in San Francisco, CA and uses the Pacific time zone to set the official eBay time.

The table below shows the difference between the time zones in the United States and eBay's official time.

Time Zone	eBay Official Time 12:00 PM (noon)	Hours Difference
Eastern	3:00 PM	+3
Central	2:00 PM	+2
Mountain	1:00 PM	+1
Pacific	12:00 PM (noon)	0
Alaska	11:00 AM	-1
Hawaii	10:00 AM	-2

HOW MUCH TIME DOES AN
AUCTION HAVE LEFT?

Critical to successful bidding is to know how much time is left in the auction. The item's auction page shows how much time remains before the auction ends.

Bidding activity increases near the end of an auction. So, if you want an item, be sure to know when the auction ends so you can make the winning bid at the last moment.

You should know that eBay's auction pages do not refresh automatically. You must manually refresh the page to display the exact time remaining in an auction. To refresh you browser, push F5 or click your browser's refresh button.

Remember that eBay uses Pacific time to specify the ending time. So an auction ending at 6:00 PM actually ends at 9:00 PM on the east coast. Be sure to convert the eBay time to your time zone.

113

WHY IS THE ITEM LOCATION IMPORTANT?

Knowing the item's location helps you determine the shipping cost and shipping time. eBay spans the globe so you need to know whether you are buying something in London, Kentucky or London, England.

If an item doesn't have a fixed shipping rate then its location becomes very important. Of course the larger the item, and the farther it must travel, the more expensive the shipping cost.

Also, items farther away will take longer to ship. However, the seller may upgrade the shipping method upon request.

Items located out of your home state will generally not have a sales tax associated with the sale. Part of the benefit of eBay is buying items without state sales tax applied.

WHAT TYPES OF PAYMENT WILL THE SELLER ACCEPT?

Generally you will find the seller's accepted payment methods at the bottom of the item's auction page. However, a seller may put the payment information in the item description, which is another reason why you should thoroughly read the description.

The seller lists the accepted payment methods at the bottom of an item's auction page. Most sellers use one or more of the following:

- PayPal.
- Personal checks (although you may have to wait for the check to clear).
- Credit Cards.
- Cash.
- Money Orders.
- Cashier checks.
- Electronic checks (e-checks).
- Bank to bank wire transfer.
- Escrow.

Most sellers use PayPal as the preferred payment method. Be sure you understand the

115

payment details before making a bid. If you don't understand how to pay, or you want more information, feel free ask the seller a question.

Remember, the seller has final say on what type of payment to accept.

WHAT IS SAFEHARBOR?

eBay has a comprehensive safe shopping resource and fraud protection team called SafeHarbor. Think of the SafeHarbor group as the eBay FBI.

The SafeHarbor team investigates selling abuses or seller rule violations. Some of the areas the group investigates are:

- Shill bidding (more on this later).
- Prohibited activities in the Feedback Forum.
- Non-paying bidders.
- Spammers.
- Prohibited items for sale.

DOES THE SELLER OFFER ESCROW?

A seller specifies if they offer escrow either in the item description or in the shipping and payments section.

If escrow is not mentioned by a seller, but you think you want to buy an item using escrow, email the seller and ask if they would be willing to use escrow. You may have to pay the escrow fees, but if it makes you feel safer about the transaction, then the fee is worth it.

We provide more details on working with escrow in Part 7.

DOES THE SELLER ACCEPT RETURNS?

Once again, a seller generally lists the return policy in the item description section.

If a seller accepts returns you will want to know if a restocking fee applies and who pays for return shipping. Be sure to understand the return policy before buying an item.

WHAT SHOULD I KNOW ABOUT BUYING ANTIQUES?

You can certainly purchase antiques on eBay. However, you should have a very good knowledge about the antique you want to purchase and buy the item from a very reputable antique dealer.

eBay provides a list of companies that can give a professional opinion on the antique, which will tell you whether or not the item is worth placing a bid. These companies do charge for their services.

In addition, you may want to have the antique verified, which means a professional inspects it and determines if it is of value. When having an item verified, the inspector will often grade the item to determine its physical condition and relative value.

Only after you collect all pertinent information should you consider bidding on a high-ticket antique. You may find a bargain on eBay, but do your homework first!

PART 6

Bidding In eBay Auctions

Once you've found the item you want to buy, you must bid on it. Don't worry; bidding on eBay is simple, fun and exciting. Just remember to keep your cool. Don't get caught up in the frenzy and overbid on an item.

In this Part we discuss how bidding on eBay auctions work. Topics we cover include proxy bidding, placing bids, bidding strategies, and paying for items.

WHAT IS PROXY BIDDING?

eBay auctions use a proxy bidding system. That is, eBay bids on your behalf up to a maximum bid amount, which you set. eBay will never bid more than your maximum amount.

Here is how proxy bidding works. You place a bid by entering the maximum amount you will pay for an item, which could be significantly more than the current bid. This is the absolute maximum amount you intend to spend on the item.

Once you submit your maximum bid, eBay, on your behalf, bids the current bid plus the minimum bid increment. If, another person bids more than your current bid, eBay acts as your proxy and submits a higher bid for you.

This process continues until the other bidder stops bidding, the current bid equals your maximum bid or the auction ends.

WHAT IS THE PROXY BIDDING PROCESS?

Here is an overview of how eBay's proxy bidding works:

1. The seller posts the item for sale, which may have a reserve price.
2. You bid on the item by entering the maximum amount you are willing to pay. eBay places a bid for you equal to the current bid plus the minimum bid increment.
3. If someone else bids, then eBay will raise your bid by the minimum bid increment unless it would exceed your maximum amount.
4. You win the item if you have the highest bid at the end of the auction.
5. eBay sends you an email congratulating you for winning.
6. You make arrangements with the seller to complete the transaction, which may include payment and shipping details.
7. The seller sends you the item after you pay.

WHAT ARE THE ADVANTAGES
OF PROXY BIDDING?

Your first thought might be; "I don't want eBay bidding for me!" which was our first thought as well. However, eBay's Proxy Bidding system has several advantages.

First, proxy bidding can save you money. If people stop bidding before your maximum amount is reached, then you only pay the current amount, not your maximum bid amount.

Secondly, proxy bidding saves you time. You can set your maximum bid and walk away. If you win, you get an email. Just be sure to regularly check your email so you can be a responsible and courteous buyer.

Lastly, proxy bidding can eliminate bidding errors. When eBay bids for you it will not enter a bid of $99.90 instead of $9.99. A simple typing or keystroke error can easily happen when a person enters a bid.

WHAT IS THE MINIMUM BID INCREMENT?

eBay has policies on the minimum amount you must increase your bid. They will not let you raise a bid by $0.01. You must bid the current price plus the minimum bid increment, which is the smallest amount that you can increase a bid. eBay bases the minimum bid increment using the current bid on the item. The chart below shows the bid increments:

Current Price	Bid Increment
$0.01–$0.99	$0.05
$1.00–$4.99	$0.25
$5.00–$24.99	$0.50
$25.00–$99.99	$1.00
$100.00–$249.99	$2.50
$250.00–$499.99	$5.00
$500.00–$999.99	$10.00
$1000.00–$2499.99	$25.00
$2500.00–$4999.99	$50.00
$5000.00 and up	$100.00

HOW DOES THE MINIMUM BID INCREMENT WORK?

The minimum bid increment specifies how much you must increase the current bid.

Here's an example:

Suppose the current bid is $5.00 for an item. From the table on the previous page you see that the minimum bid increment is $0.50. Therefore, the next acceptable bid is $5.50, which the current bid ($5.00) plus the minimum bid increment ($0.50).

HOW DO I BID ON AN ITEM?

You can enter a bid in two places; at the bottom of the item auction page in the "Ready To Bid" section or by clicking the **Place Bid** button located under the item's current bid.

The text box in the "Ready to Bid" section allows you to enter your maximum bid, which must be greater than or equal to the amount listed beside the text box. You can also leave it blank and click the **Place Bid** button to enter a bid on the next page.

Clicking the **Place Bid** button opens the "Place Your Bid" page, which has a text box for you to enter a bid. To bid, enter the maximum amount you wish to pay and click the **Continue** button.

Next a confirmation page appears. eBay asks you to enter your password to verify that you really want to bid.

Be sure to read the warning, which states that a bid is a contract to buy the item if you win.

Important — Do not submit a bid unless you are serious about buying an item!

eBay will send you an email to confirm your bid. Review it carefully and treat it as a receipt.

HOW DO I VIEW THE BID HISTORY?

You might find it interesting to view the bid history for an auction.

To view the bid history, click on the Bids link next to the "History" label on the auction page.

The bid history page shows you the members who have bid on the item. The bid history page does not list the bid values, only those who made bids

You can view information about the bidder by clicking their User ID. You can also see what type of items they buy and what type of feedback they leave.

DOES A RESERVE PRICE AFFECT BIDDING?

A reserve price does not directly affect the bidding process. That is, you can set your maximum bid lower than the reserve price. For instance, you may have the highest bid at the end of an auction, but if it is below the reserve, you do not win the item.

A reserve price only sets the minimum price that a seller will accept for an item. Remember, on auctions with reserves, the final bid must exceed the reserve price before the seller must sell the item.

Until the current bid equals or exceeds the reserve amount, then you will see the "Reserve Not Met" notice. When the current bid exceeds the reserve you will see the "Reserve Met" message beside the current bid.

WHAT ARE SOME BIDDING STRATEGIES?

Below are some strategies you can try when bidding for items:

- To save money, don't budge from your maximum bid amount. If someone outbids you, then try bidding on another item at the price you want to pay.

- Enter your maximum bid plus $0.80. For example, if you would pay $1,000 for an item, make your maximum bid $1,000.80. If someone tries to sneak past you with a bid of $1,000.50, you still win!

- Most bidding occurs in the final few minutes of an auction. If you really want an item, then be available at the last minute to sneak in the winning bid.

WHAT ABOUT TIE BIDS?

eBay obeys the first come, first served rule. If two people enter the same maximum bid, the first to do so wins the item.

To reduce the chance of a tie bid, try adding a few cents to your maximum bid amount. This technique helps ensure your bid is unique. Many people may bid $6.00, but very few may bid $6.03.

WHAT IS AN OUTBID NOTICE?

eBay sends you an "Outbid Notice" email when you have the highest bid on an item then another person outbids you.

In the email there is a link that lets you place a higher bid. If you want to place another bid, just click the link.

If you do not want to place a higher bid, do nothing!

WHAT IS THE END OF AUCTION EMAIL?

eBay sends an "End of Auction" email to all bidders who participated in an auction but did not win. The email informs you that you did not win the item and that the auction is over.

The email also has links to similar auctions. So if you didn't win this item, you can try another auction.

WHAT IS SNIPING?

Sniping is a bidding technique where you wait until the last few seconds of an auction then submit a bid that you think will win.

Some people believe that eBay forbids sniping. But they don't. They specifically address sniping and say that it is part of the eBay experience.

Sniping can frustrate some bidders who had their hopes set on winning an item. Don't worry though, if you really want an item, snipe it! Just don't get upset when you get sniped.

WHAT IS SNIPING SOFTWARE?

Some companies produce software that will snipe auctions for you.

The programs work much in the same way as eBay's proxy bidding system, except it watches the auction's ending time as well. When an auction nears completion, the software submits a bid for you.

You might find sniping software useful for auctions that end in the middle of the night or while you are at work.

You can purchase sniping software at your local computer store or over the Internet.

WHAT IS A DUTCH AUCTION?

Proxy auctions are used for single items. Dutch Auctions are used to sell multiple identical items. As you might expect, they work a little differently than single item auctions.

For example, a seller may run a Dutch Auction for 20 gold chains with hopes of selling the whole lot.

When bidding in a Dutch Auction you enter both the number of items you want to buy and the amount you will pay for a single item. For example, you might want to buy two gold chains at $20 each, for a total of $40.

Unlike proxy auctions, everyone pays the same price for the item. Unless all items are bid on, the lowest successful bid wins.

So, if our gold chain seller receives bids on all 20 chains, you get your two for your bid of $20 each.

Continuing with the gold chains example, if only eight chains are bid on, and there was a bid $10 before you, then you win your chains for $10, not $20. You just saved $10 per gold chain!

There's a little more to Dutch Auctions than described in this brief overview. Visit eBay's Services page for more information on how Dutch Auctions (Multiple Auctions) work.

WHAT SHOULD I KNOW ABOUT DUTCH AUCTION BIDDING?

Dutch Auction bidding differs from proxy auctions in several ways:

- Bids are not secret so everyone knows what and when everyone else bid. The Winning Bidders List shows the current successful bidders. The Bid History link is located on the Winning Bidders page.
- Your bid price is listed as a total and not the amount for one item. If you bid $20 on two gold chains then eBay shows your bid as $40.
- Every bidder pays the same amount, which is the lowest successful bid.

DOES AN AUCTION PAGE
UPDATE AUTOMATICALLY?

Auction pages do not update automatically. You must manually update the page by clicking on the browser's Refresh button.

With Internet Explorer, you can click View then Refresh on the menu bar. You can also press F5 as a shortcut to refresh the page.

Some keyboards require the function keys (F1–F9) to be turned on in order to work properly. Check your keyboard operating instructions if you are having problems with the function keys.

CAN I RETRACT A BID?

As a rule, eBay considers a bid as a binding contract, except for some very special cases.

Here are a few examples of when eBay MAY let you retract a bid:

- You mistyped a bid. For example you enter $99.90 instead of $9.99.
- The seller drastically changes the item description during the middle of the auction.
- You cannot reach the seller after reasonable attempts.
- Someone has used your User ID to bid on an item.

eBay has bid retraction procedures posted under the Services section. You can also get more information on bid retraction from the eBay help system.

WHAT IS SHILL BIDDING?

Shill bidding is the intentional placing of bids, by you or an acquaintance, to raise the price of an item.

For example, a seller's friend, or family member, may bid on an item then retract it, just to raise the current price.

Shill bidding is illegal and prohibited. People have gone to prison for shill bidding on eBay.

If you suspect suspicious bidding activity, do not hesitate to report it to the eBay staff. Helping to keep eBay safe is the responsibility of every member.

PART 7

Completing The Transaction

Congratulations! You won an eBay auction. Hopefully you got a great bargain. Now you might be wondering what's next.

In this Part we walk you through the process of completing an eBay transaction. We cover what to do when you win, how to pay and how to inspect your item.

143

WHAT HAPPENS WHEN I WIN AN AUCTION?

When you win an auction, eBay sends you an "End of Auction" email that contains everything you need to know to complete the transaction. You should review the email closely.

Hopefully the seller uses eBay's payment system (more on this later). If so, you may receive an email with the following:

- Total price you owe which includes any shipping costs or applicable tax.
- A **Pay Now** button which will take you to eBay's payment system.
- Seller contact information.
- Seller payment requirements and timeline.

You will also find information concerning how to pay and contact the seller on the item auction page after you win the item.

WHAT ARE MY DUTIES AS A WINNING BIDDER?

Congratulations! You won an eBay auction and got a great bargain. But now what? Your biggest responsibility as a winning bidder is to communicate with the seller.

Upon winning you should contact the seller and specify when and how you will pay for your item. This gives the seller some confidence that you are legitimate.

Next, do what you say and pay for the item. Don't procrastinate or you risk getting negative feedback. After paying, you may want to contact the seller to arrange specific shipping methods.

Remember, communicating and keeping your word will lead to a successful eBay transaction and a great reputation.

WHY SHOULD I CONTACT THE SELLER?

One of the main rules on eBay is that buyers and sellers must communicate. The seller wants to know that you actually intend to purchase the item. Of course, after paying you want to hear from the seller to know when he will ship the item.

Therefore, after winning an auction, you should inform the seller about how and when you intend to pay. You can also provide some specific shipping instructions if needed.
Don't wait for the seller to contact you. Being proactive will help you build a favorable eBay reputation.

HOW DO I PAY FOR AN ITEM?

How you pay depends upon the type of payment the seller will take. Some eBay sellers only accept PayPal. Some sellers, especially commercial entities doing business on eBay accept checks, money orders, credit cards, as well as PayPal.

If accepted, PayPal provides the fastest and easiest payment method. It is also the safest. As we mentioned, PayPal is free to the buyer and the seller pays a small processing fee.

If the seller takes checks or money orders, hurry and mail the payment to them. Be sure to send an email to the seller to let them know the payment is on its way.

WHAT WILL I OWE FOR SHIPPING AND HANDLING?

The shipping and handling costs vary from item to item. Generally, small items have fixed rates, while larger items have variable rates. The final cost depends upon:

- **Size** — heavy and large items cost more to ship.
- **Value** — expensive items often have shipping insurance that increases the shipping price.
- **Distance** — items located further away cost more to ship.
- **Time** — shipping overnight or with second day air costs more than standard ground.

The seller usually chooses the shipping method and posts it in the item's description. If you don't like the shipping option, or want a lower cost method, contact the seller and ask if they will change it.

Some auctions do not list shipping and handling charges because the amount will depend on how and where the item is shipped. If this is the case, promptly contact the seller to determine the cost.

Some sellers have a shipping calculator on their listing page to give you an idea of shipping costs.

WHAT IS THE EBAY PAYMENT SYSTEM?

eBay's payment system provides a way for a buyer and seller to easily complete a transaction.

The payment system automatically sends emails to both the buyer and seller with payment and shipping information. It also supports eBay's Checkout feature, which further simplifies the transaction process.

A seller does not have to use the eBay payment system. If the system is not used then parties must exchange the pertinent information to complete the transaction. However, because of its ease and integration, most eBay sellers use the payment system.

WHAT IS THE CHECKOUT FEATURE?

eBay's Checkout feature is a one-stop payment solution for buyers and sellers. The system uses eBay's information about you and the seller to streamline the purchase process.

For example, when you buy an item, the seller receives your current shipping address from the eBay system. This saves you from having to send it to the seller and also ensures accuracy.

To use the Checkout feature, just click the **Checkout** button located on the item's auction page after it expires. Clicking the button takes you to eBay's payment system.

The Checkout feature also lets the seller email you an invoice for the item, which has a **Pay Now** button on it as well.

Not all auctions utilize the Checkout Feature. The seller must explicitly enable the option when listing the item for sale. Also, the seller must accept PayPal to use the Checkout feature.

WHAT DO I DO ONCE I RECEIVE MY ITEM?

What you do now has a great impact on your eBay reputation.

As soon as the item arrives, you should carefully open and inspect the item. If it looks acceptable, test it. If it passes the test, email the seller and tell them all is well.

Sometimes you may not be able to get to this in a timely manner. At a minimum, email the seller and tell them the item arrived and that you intend to open, inspect, and test the item at a later date. Then make sure you stick to your timetable.

SHOULD I LEAVE FEEDBACK ABOUT THE SELLER?

You should always leave feedback on members after an eBay transaction. As a buyer you should rate the seller's performance.

Here are some factors to evaluate:

- Was the item description accurate?
- Did the seller ship the item in a timely manner?
- Was the seller pleasant and easy to work with?
- Did the item arrive on-time and undamaged?

Remember, eBay relies on feedback to work successfully. Without feedback, members would not be able to check another member's behavior.

WHAT ABOUT BAIT AND SWITCH?

Yes, it has happened on eBay. A member bought one thing and got something else.

If this happens to you, contact the seller immediately. Explain the problem and see if they made a mistake. If so, be flexible and work with the seller to correct the problem.

Contact eBay if the seller does not respond or correct the problem. The Services page has lots of information on buyer protection plans and the steps to take if you think you are a victim of fraud.

WHAT ARE EBAY'S BUYER PROTECTION PLANS?

Rest assured, eBay wants a safe trading environment. Its continued success depends on it. However, eBay realizes that all sellers are not trustworthy.

If your best efforts to communicate with the seller fail, you can try to use one of eBay's Buyer Protection Plans. These plans may help you recover some loss only if the item never arrived, or the item was significantly misrepresented. However, you cannot receive compensation for an item you do not like.

To that end, eBay provides the following two protection plans:

- **Standard Purchase Protection Program** — this program provides reimbursement up to $200 for qualifying transactions. This program applies to every eBay auction.
- **PayPal Buyer Protection** — this PayPal program covers losses up to $500. However, it is only available on auctions conducted by qualified sellers and for payments made with PayPal.

You can find more information on both protection plans on eBay's Services web page.

WHAT IS ESCROW PROTECTION?

Escrow is a way to reduce potential fraud by using a third party to collect and hold money until an eBay transaction completes.

The seller benefits because the escrow company ensures the buyer has sufficient funds to purchase the item. The buyer benefits because the escrow company allows them to inspect and accept the item before paying the seller.

Buyer and sellers typically use an escrow service for very expensive items such as jewelry, antiques, and motor vehicles.

One important note, eBay only endorses www.escrow.com to perform escrow services. Be wary of any seller who uses another escrow agency.

There are fees associated with using www.escrow.com. Usually the buyer and seller determine who will pay the fees before beginning the transaction.

HOW DOES ESCROW WORK?

Before using escrow, a buyer and seller must agree to use it for the transaction. Both parties must also agree who will pay the escrow fees and which escrow service to use.

Again, eBay strongly recommends to use www.escrow.com as the escrow agent. A typical escrow transaction proceeds as follows:

1. The buyer sends payment to www.escrow.com instead of the seller. The buyer must contact www.escrow.com to determine acceptable payment methods.
2. The seller sends the item to the buyer. To ensure delivery, www.escrow.com tracks the shipment to the buyer.
3. Once the buyer receives, inspects, and accepts the item, www.escrow.com sends payment to the seller to complete the transaction.
4. If the buyer rejects the item for a legitimate reason, they must ship it back to the seller before the payment is returned.

PART 8

Selling On eBay

Are you cleaning out your closet, or downsizing your household? You might consider selling some your unwanted items on eBay. It's easier than you think.

In this Part we help you learn the basics about selling items on eBay. We start with how to sign-up as a seller and end with how to ship the item to the buyer.

After reading this Part you will be ready to begin selling on eBay!

WHAT IS THE EBAY SELLING PROCESS?

Selling on eBay is simple. Here is an overview of the selling process:

1. If you are not a registered seller, you must first set up a free Seller's Account.
2. Write an Item Description for what you want to sell.
3. Take a photograph of the item.
4. List the item using eBay's "Sell Your Item Form."
5. Sell the item to the highest bidder.
6. Receive payment from the winner.
7. Pack and ship the item to the winner.
8. Leave feedback about the transaction.

We provide more details on the selling process in the rest of this Part.

WHAT DO I NEED TO SETUP A SELLER'S ACCOUNT?

Setting up a sellers account requires the following three things:

- An eBay account.
- A method to receive money when you sell an item.
- A method to pay eBay's auction fees.

If you are not an eBay member, you must create a member account first. Part 3 walks you through this process.

To accept payments you need a bank account or PayPal account. As you probably know by now, eBay owns PayPal and recommends that you use the service. PayPal provides excellent service and security. You should use it unless you have a good reason not too.

Unlike buying, selling on eBay is not free. There are some small fees associated with listing and selling items. To pay the fees, eBay can either withdraw the amount from a bank account or charge a credit card. It is your preference.

HOW DO I SETUP A SELLER'S ACCOUNT?

To set up a seller's account just click the <u>Sell</u> link on the eBay Menu.

eBay first checks to see if you have a Seller's Account. If you do not have one, then eBay starts the account setup process. You should have either a credit card or checkbook handy to expedite this process.

The first step of the process is to verify your personal information such as your address and phone number. Next, eBay asks for a credit card to verify your identity. To reduce problems with fraud, eBay tries to ensure that everyone is who they say they are.

eBay does not bill your card for anything; it only uses your card to make sure you are a real person. You can also use Equifax's ID Verify for a nominal fee.

Lastly, you must choose how you want to pay the auction fees. You can either let eBay charge your credit card or withdraw the funds from a bank account. We suggest using a credit card as it will help you better track your selling activity.

WHY DO I NEED A CREDIT CARD
TO SELL ON EBAY?

eBay requires a credit card for two reasons. First, eBay uses it to verify your identity. It does not charge a fee to become a seller. Your credit card is only used to verify your identity.

Second, eBay uses your credit card to pay your auction fees. Although you can elect to have the fees withdrawn directly from your bank account instead of using your credit card.

Be glad eBay goes to great lengths to verify a seller's identity. If it didn't then the chances of fraudulent sellers signing up would increase. eBay verifies everyone's identity for everyone's protection.

WHAT IS ID VERIFY?

If you prefer eBay not use your credit card or bank account to verify your identity, then you can use Equifax's service called ID Verify.

Equifax is a world-wide financial services company that can verify your identity for a small fee. The company checks your identity using your credit history and personal information from public records.

To use Equifax's service when creating a seller's account, just click the <u>ID Verify</u> link on the Verify Your Identity page.

WHAT ARE EBAY'S SELLING FEES?

Although opening a Seller's account is free, selling items on eBay is not.

Nonetheless, eBay's fees are competitive with newspaper classified ads. However, eBay provides international exposure versus the local exposure of most newspapers or trading posts.

The following list summarizes eBay's fees:

- **Insertion fee** — due when you initially list an item.
- **Final value fee** — due only if you sell an item.
- **Picture fee** — an optional fee charged only if you use more than one picture.
- **Listing upgrade fee(s)** — an optional fee(s) associated with listing enhancements such as a bold title or highlighted listing.
- **PayPal fees** — a required fee due only when you sell an item and use PayPal to collect the payment.

Remember, eBay either charges your credit card or debits your bank account for these fees.

WHAT IS THE INSERTION FEE?

Just like a newspaper charges a fee to list a classified ad, eBay charges you an insertion fee to list an item.

The fee amount depends upon the starting price for the item. You must pay this fee whether your item sells or not.

The table below shows eBay's current insertion fees.

Starting or Reserve Price	Insertion Fee
$0.01–$0.99	$0.30
$1.00–$9.99	$0.35
$10.00–$24.99	$0.60
$25.00–$49.99	$1.20
$50.00–$199.99	$2.40
$200.00–$499.99	$3.60
$500.00 or more	$4.80

Be sure to check the eBay's Services web page for more details on the current insertion fees.

WHAT IS THE FINAL VALUE FEE?

eBay also charges a small fee, called the final value fee, when you sell your item. An auction's winning bid determines this fee.

Like the other fees, the amount is nominal. You do not pay a final value fee if a reserve price is not met or the item doesn't sell. The table below shows eBay's current final value fees.

Closing Price	Final Value Fee
Item not sold	No Fee
$1.00–$25.00	5.25% of the closing value
$25.01–$1,000.00	5.25% of the initial $25.00 ($1.31), plus 2.75% of the remaining closing value balance ($25.01–$1,000.00)
Over $1,000.01	5.25% of the initial $25.00 ($1.31), plus 2.75% of the initial $25.01–$1,000.00 ($26.81), plus 1.50% of the remaining closing value balance ($1,000.01–closing value)

Be sure to check eBay's Services web page for more details on the current final value fees.

165

WHAT IS THE PICTURE SERVICES FEE?

Almost all sellers use pictures to help sell their items so eBay gives you one free photo with each auction. If you use more than one photo there will be an extra cost.

To help sellers effectively use pictures in their auction, eBay provides a Picture Service at an extra cost.

Besides allowing you to use more than one picture, eBay's Picture Service provides you with options on how to present your pictures. For example, you can use two or more pictures to create a slide show. Or you can show the details of an item with a super-sized view.

Check the Services web page for more information on eBay's Picture Services.

WHAT ARE LISTING UPGRADE FEES?

The default eBay auction uses simple text and a single picture. Don't misunderstand; you can certainly sell items using the default eBay listing. To help catch a buyer's eye you can "upgrade" your listing.

Some examples of eBay's upgrade options include:

- Bold text for the item title.
- "Buy It Now" feature.
- Highlighting of the auction in search listings.
- Subtitles to further describe your item.
- Featured Item presentation.

eBay charges a small fee for each upgrade. If you really want to sell your item, consider upgrading the listing so it stands apart from the crowd.

WHAT SHOULD I CHARGE FOR SHIPPING AND HANDLING?

What you charge for shipping and handling depends upon the item, where you ship it and how you ship it.

As a rule, larger items that require special handling have higher shipping and handling fees. Smaller items tend to have lower fees.

Here are some issues to consider when setting the fee:

- Is the item big and bulky?
- Does the item require special packaging or handling?
- Is the item valuable?
- Is the item fragile?
- Do you need to use a carrier with a tracking system?
- How much does the item weigh?
- How fast does the customer want the item?

Only after you consider these factors can you determine what you should charge for shipping and handling.

SHOULD I OFFER SHIPPING INSURANCE?

Once again, whether you offer shipping insurance depends upon the item you are selling.

As a rule, you should probably offer shipping insurance for high value items, electronics or fragile items. However, it is ultimately your decision on whether or not to offer insurance.

Sometimes it might be good business to offer shipping insurance. Keep in mind that you can pass the cost of shipping insurance on to the buyer, especially if they request it.

Even if the buyer doesn't want insurance, you might consider purchasing it anyhow to ensure compensation should the item arrive broken.

HOW DO I DETERMINE THE MINIMUM BID?

Determining the minimum bid requires under-standing the market for your item. You don't want to price the item too high so bidders do not start bidding. You also don't want to set the minimum bid so low the final bid doesn't reach your expectations.

When setting your minimum bid, it's best to start by researching similar items that have sold on eBay. For instance, try to determine the demand for the item by seeing how many bids were placed during a similar auction. Look at an item's bid history page for this information.

Also, if you have time, watch a few auctions of similar items. In particular, note the minimum bid and the final bid. If you can spot a typical minimum bid for the same item then use it.

Remember, the goal is to choose a minimum bid that encourages bidding. Once someone places the first bid, others will follow.

SHOULD I USE A RESERVE PRICE?

Most eBay sellers set a minimum bid and shy away from reserve pricing.

Why? Because the bidders cannot see the reserve price and the associated secrecy often scares them away. After all, why should someone spend time bidding on an item in which they may have the highest bid but still not win the auction because the bid was below the reserve price? Ultimately, eBay members want openness, not secrecy.

Therefore, avoid a reserve price and set the minimum bid to the absolute lowest price you will accept. That way you openly state your minimum price, which, oddly enough generates more bids.

SHOULD I INCLUDE A PHOTOGRAPH
WITH THE AUCTION?

Absolutely! Buyers want to see the item they are bidding on. Only very few items, such as recipes or tickets, do not require a photograph. Even then, a small picture can help attract a bidders' attention.

In fact, you should try to include as many photos as you can. Take pictures from different angles and different lighting. Use your photographs to enhance your item's description. Don't try to be overly creative, just take good simple photos.

More importantly take pictures of any blemishes or imperfections that the item might have. Bidders demand to know what they are buying. You will definitely create an unhappy customer if you hide any imperfections.

For tips on digital photography check out our book *The Senior's Guide to Digital Photography*.

WHAT TYPE OF PICTURE SHOULD I TAKE?

eBay can only accept digital image files for use in an auction. Therefore, you should take a digital photograph of your item. If you don't have a digital camera, now is a good time to invest in one. You don't need anything expensive, just something that can produce medium quality digital prints.

You still have several options for creating a digital image if don't have a digital camera. You can have a photo lab create a digital photo from a film picture. Or you can scan a photo into your computer if you have a scanner. You can use any of these image files in your auction.

However, you are better off starting with a digital photo taken with a digital camera.

HOW CAN I IMPROVE MY DIGITAL PICTURES?

The pictures of your item can make or break your auction. However you don't have to be a professional photographer to take pictures that will help your auction succeed.

Follow these tips to produce top-notch photos:

- Take pictures in well-lit areas and always with indirect lighting.
- If indoors, try to use extra lighting to avoid the flash, which can cause unwanted reflections on glass or jewelry.
- Make sure you have a clean, neat background.
- Take color pictures.
- Take pictures of your item from different angles.
- Take pictures showing the good and bad points of your item.

For pointers on buying a digital camera and taking great pictures, read our book, *The Senior's Guide to Digital Photography*.

HOW DO I FORMAT MY PICTURES?

eBay only accepts JPEG or GIF file formats. Make sure you convert your images to either format or eBay will reject your photo.

Also try to keep your file size to less then 50 KB (kilobytes). The smaller size allows your auction page to load quickly in the buyer's web browser.

You will need to use photo-editing software to reduce the file size. Products such as Adobe's Photoshop Elements, Jasc's PaintShop Pro, or Microsoft's Picture It! have tools to create web-optimized photos.

WHAT IS AN IMAGE HOSTING SERVICE?

If you have a lot of photos that you want to use in your auction then you might consider using an image hosting service. These companies provide online storage of your images so you can link to them from an auction page.

The upside of using external image hosting is that you can reference numerous images without eBay's extra cost per image. These companies usually charge a smaller fee, on a per image basis, than eBay.

The downside of using external image hosting is that you must know HTML (the code that formats a web page) to access the images. You also have to manage another account, which means more administrative work.

We recommend using eBay's Picture Services until you become a very proficient seller. eBay has integrated their service into the auction process, and as a result it works flawlessly and has minimal overhead.

WHAT DO I NEED TO INCLUDE IN AN ITEM LISTING?

The best way to learn what you need to include in a listing is to review other auctions. Spend time looking at other auctions selling similar items so you can gain an idea about what you need for a listing.

At a minimum, an eBay listing includes:

- A detailed item description.
- One or more pictures of the item.
- Shipping and handling information.
- Accepted forms of payment.

We recommend that you get everything organized before starting the listing process, which consists of filling out eBay's "Sell Your Item" form. The process is simple, but you need to be prepared before starting.

HOW DO I WRITE AN ITEM DESCRIPTION?

The perfect item description answers all of a bidder's questions and makes a great first impression. A detailed item description will help the bidder make an informed decision and save you time by not having to answer email questions.

So what does a good item description contain? The answer, of course, depends upon the item. At a minimum include:

- The name of the item
- The manufacturer of the item.
- The make and model number of the item.
- The age and quality of the item.
- Why you want to sell the item.
- What makes the item desirable.

Furthermore, use proper sentence structure in the description. All those rules of English composition you learned long ago, really do matter.

Ultimately, you're trying to make two impressions with your description. The first is that it is a great item to buy. Secondly, you are a great person to do business with. If you make these two impressions the chances of you having a successful auction increase dramatically.

DO I NEED TO KNOW HTML?

You do not need to know HTML to write an item description. Simple text works fine for most auctions.

However, if you want to create dynamic, eye catching auction pages then you will want to learn something about HTML.

Fortunately, eBay's popularity has sparked companies to create software tools that help you create item descriptions. These programs do not cost a lot and can greatly improve your auctions appearance.

eBay provides a free tool called TurboLister that includes a HTML editor. It integrates very well with the eBay site to make creating auctions easier.

Just remember though, a lot of people have sold items using the standard eBay auction format. Unless you feel a real desire to spice up your pages, then you should probably stick with the standard format.

WHAT IS TURBOLISTER?

eBay provides free listing software called TurboLister. This tool has a lot of features that can help you create and manage your auctions.

For example, TurboLister allows you to:

- Schedule your listings to occur at a future time.
- Create attractive item descriptions with a HTML editor.
- Save default values for the selling options you use most.
- Preview your listing before submitting it to eBay.

Although the tool is free, you are still responsible for all listing fees associated with running an auction. Nonetheless, as a free tool, TurboLister can help you become a "turbo seller" in no time!

WHAT IS THE SELL YOUR ITEM FORM?

Just as you fill out a form to place an item in the newspaper's classified section, you fill out a form to list an item in an eBay auction.

The "Sell Your Item" form isn't a piece of paper, but a series of web pages similar to those you completed to become a member and open a seller's account.

The form walks you through the process of entering your item description, uploading pictures, listing the shipping and handling fees and specifying your accepted payments.

To make the process smooth and quick it is very important to have all the information ready before starting to list an item.

HOW LONG DOES IT TAKE TO BEFORE MY ITEM APPEARS ON EBAY?

It happens immediately! As soon as you click the **Submit Listing** button, the item becomes available for sale on eBay.

On the "Congratulations" page you will find a link to the item so you can review it.

CAN I CHANGE THE ITEM DESCRIPTION AFTER MY AUCTION BEGINS?

Oops! When admiring your newly created auction you notice a misspelled word or missing information. Don't despair; eBay will let you correct the problem.

You can change almost anything about the listing if no bids have been placed. Just go to the item description page and click the <u>Revise Item</u> link on the top section of the item page. Follow the instructions from there.

If you already have bids on the item, then you can only modify the item description. Go to the Selling tab on the "My eBay" page, then click on the <u>Add to my description</u> link. From here you can enhance the description, add pictures, or correct mistakes.

CAN I END MY AUCTION EARLY?

As a seller you have the right to end your auction early.

To stop an in-progress auction, go to the Seller Services section of the "My eBay" page and click the End my auction early link. You will need the item number to continue.

eBay also requires you to cancel all active bids before ending the auction. As a professional courtesy you should also send the bidders an email stating that you have canceled the auction.

WHAT ARE COUNTERS?

Counters show how many unique visitors have viewed your auction.

As a seller you can use a counter to determine how much interest you have in an item. Having a lot of page views but very few bids might indicate that you need to change the item description or lower the starting bid.

As a buyer, counters let you know the demand for an item and if a lot of bidders will be competing for the item.

You can find the counter at the bottom of the item's auction page.

WHAT ARE SOME ITEM TITLE TIPS?

A key to successful selling is to help bidders find your item. Creating an effective title provides a way for bidders to quickly locate your item among the millions of other eBay items.

To understand why the title is important you should consider buyer behavior. More often than not, eBay buyers quickly scan item titles looking for what they desire. Therefore, you only have a few seconds to catch their eye with your title.

The following list provides a few hints on creating effective titles:

- Use accurate, descriptive keywords to describe the item.
- Include the brand and model number.
- Spell words correctly.
- Avoid words like WOW! or LOOK! Bidders don't search on those words, so do not waste the space.

HOW SHOULD I SHIP THE ITEM?

The best and safest way to ship an item to a buyer is to use a carrier that offers package tracking. Almost all major carriers offer this service. A few you should consider include FedEx, UPS, U.S. Postal Service, and Airborne Express.

Having a way to track the package places both you and the buyer at ease. The buyer knows the item has shipped and you know when the buyer received the item.

HOW SHOULD I PACK THE ITEM FOR SHIPPING?

Above all else, pack the item so it doesn't become damaged during shipment. Of course, the item dictates the packing. Fragile items such as glass require different packaging than a hammer.

If you are only selling a few items, you might consider using a shipping service that will pack and ship the item for a small fee. You might also want to consider this option if you do not have time or the materials to correctly pack the item.

The appearance of the shipping container and packing material is important. Using a beat-up box and shredded newspaper may give the buyer a bad first impression of the product. Be sure to use quality containers and materials.

If you need boxes and bubble wrap, consider buying it on eBay. Buying these items on eBay can also help you earn positive feedback.

WHAT IS THE RELIST FEATURE?

If your item doesn't sell, eBay provides you with a way to quickly list your item again using the Relist feature.

In fact eBay may waive the relisting fee if your item sells the second time. Below are the criteria for having the listing fee waived:

- If the item had a reserve price, you must specify a lower reserve than the original auction.
- You must specify a lower opening bid than the original auction.

Under the Seller Services section of the item's description page you will find the link, <u>Relist this item</u>. Clicking it takes you to a Relisting page. Just follow the instructions to start another auction.

CAN BIDDERS RETRACT THEIR BID?

Yes, bidders may retract their bids. However, they may only do so under certain circumstances.

For instance, a bid retraction is allowed if the bidder entered the wrong bid amount. Bid retraction is also allowed if you significantly change the item description during the auction.

eBay treats every bid as a contract and frowns on bid retraction. A member's Feedback tracks all bid retractions. For what its worth, eBay investigates chronic bid retraction behavior and could suspend or remove abusive members who abuse this privilege.

CAN I CANCEL BIDS ON MY AUCTION?

As a seller you have the right to cancel any member's bid in your auction. However, eBay discourages this practice.

Only under the following two circumstances should you consider canceling a bid:

- The buyer asks that you cancel his bid. As a professional courtesy you should honor his request.
- You have a bidder with a considerable amount of negative feedback. Be sure to fully review before canceling the bid.

WHAT ARE THE BEST AUCTION ENDING TIMES AND DAYS?

Most bidding for an auction occurs in the final few minutes. Therefore you want to determine the best date and time to end an auction for your target market. The availability of bidders ultimately determines the best time for an auction to end.

If you are targeting younger buyers, then ending an auction at 10:00 PM on a Friday or Saturday night is not prudent. Likewise if you are selling to an older crowd, auctions ending past 10:00 PM on any night may not fare so well.

To pick the best ending time for your auction you should study how similar items have best sold on eBay. In particular note which items sold for the highest prices and what time the auction ended. This will give you an idea of when to end your auction.

WHAT HAPPENS AFTER I SELL MY ITEM?

Be a professional! That is, be kind, courteous, respectful and responsive to the buyer. If you act professionally, chances are the buyer will too.

When you sell your item, contact the buyer as soon as you can. In your email restate your accepted payment methods and shipping policy. This helps ensure everyone understands the terms of the sale. If you use eBay's payment services these emails are sent automatically.

You should also provide links to any payment service you want to use. This added convenience might encourage the buyer to pay faster.

Lastly, sincerely thank them for purchasing the item and let them know you will ship immediately after you receive payment.

HOW DO I ACCEPT PAYMENT?

If you let the buyer use PayPal to pay with a credit card, then you will receive your money as soon as the buyer pays.

Once the money is in your PayPal account then it is safe to send the item to the buyer.

If you accept other forms of payment then arrange with the buyer on how to complete the transaction. If the buyer is paying by check, remind him that the check must clear before you will send the item.

WHAT IF MY BIDDER DOESN'T RESPOND TO EMAIL?

First, don't panic or assume you've been ripped off. After all, you still own the item.

Please remember that a buyer is human and sometimes emergencies arise; such as a loved one may become sick or they are called out of town with work. You would appreciate some leeway in similar circumstances.

If you don't hear back from the buyer within a day then you should resend the email. If you still don't hear from the buyer, then call them. If you do speak with the buyer, be polite and courteous.

If you have made a valiant effort to contact the buyer, but did not have any success, then you should report the buyer to eBay. It's good practice to send a last-chance warning email to the buyer stating that you are reporting him to eBay.

WHAT IS THE SECOND CHANCE OFFER?

If you cannot contact the buyer, or they back out of the transaction, you can try eBay's Second Chance Offer feature.

Briefly, this feature allows you offer the item to another bidder when the winning bidder fails to buy the item.

You can learn more about the Second Chance Offer feature by clicking the selling tab on your "My eBay" page.

WHAT SHOULD I NOT DO AFTER THE SALE?

If you find yourself stuck with an unresponsive buyer do not lose your professionalism. This means do not:

- Berate or scold the buyer.
- Criticize the buyer for being unresponsive.
- Lecture the buyer on why they should respond.
- Hassle the buyer with phone calls or excessive emails.

Always be professional and give the bidder the benefit of the doubt. Who knows, the buyer may have become sick or was in an accident. Allow the transaction to continue for some reasonable time before ending it. You can always leave negative feedback about the buyer, which hurts the most within the eBay Community.

SHOULD I LEAVE FEEDBACK
ABOUT THE BUYER?

You should always leave feedback on members after an eBay transaction. As a seller you should rate the buyer's behavior during the transaction.

Remember, eBay relies on feedback to work successfully. Without feedback, members would not be able to check another member's behavior.

WHO LEAVES FEEDBACK FIRST?

This is a question with no clear answer.

However, as a seller, you may aspire to reach the elusive PowerSeller status or next selling tier. Both of which rely on positive feedback.

So, most eBay sellers agree that as the seller, you should leave feedback first. This may prompt the bidder to leave feedback on you.

WHAT SHOULD FEEDBACK SAY?

As a seller you should rate the buyer on their responsibilities in the transaction, which are to pay in full and on-time. If the buyer does this, then you should give them positive feedback.

Keep feedback short, simple, direct and upbeat. Examples of appropriate positive feedback are:

- "Great buyer, timely and responsive!"
- "A reputable eBay buyer, fast payer and easy to work with."
- "Highly recommended buyer, great to do business with!"

WHEN SHOULD I LEAVE NEGATIVE FEEDBACK?

Negative feedback on eBay is equivalent to a black eye. Think long and hard before leaving negative feedback as it will tarnish a member's reputation. However, if negative feedback is warranted, do not hesitate to give them negative feedback. The eBay Community appreciates honest feedback.

The guiding rule is to leave negative feedback only when the buyer backed out of the deal. Leave neutral feedback if the transaction was less than positive.

Some examples of negative feedback include:

- "Hard to do business with. Doesn't pay."
- "Unable to contact bidder, recommend avoiding."
- "Not a serious buyer, never received payment."

WHAT SHOULD FEEDBACK NOT SAY?

Like a good eBay seller, always leave professional feedback.

Don't leave feedback with foul or abusive language. Also, avoid calling the seller names or otherwise insulting them.

Non-professional feedback can hurt your reputation more than the buyer's.

50 TIPS FOR BUYING AND SELLING ON EBAY

Tips for Buying

1. Buy items close to home to minimize shipping costs.

2. Leave positive feedback about the seller only after you are satisfied with your purchase.

3. Use eBay's Site Map page to find information fast.

4. Understand eBay's Buyer Protection Plans.

5. Contact the seller when you win an auction and let them know when and how you will pay.

6. Always follow the instructions on the eBay Checkout page.

7. Sign up and pay for items with PayPal.

8. Don't hesitate to ask the seller questions about the quality of the product.

9. Look at all the pictures of an item.

10. Set up your My eBay page so you can easily monitor auctions.

11. Use the Buy It Now option when you want an item quickly.

12. Don't forget to consider the extra costs of shipping, handling, tax, and insurance when bidding on an item.

13. Summer is the slowest time on eBay so you can usually find great bargains during this season.

14. Always ask for shipping insurance if you want it.

15. Pay for your auction with a credit card as some companies offer fraud protection in addition to eBay's standard protection.

16. If paying by check, write the auction number and item description on the check.

17. Print the auction page for an easy reference.

18. Thoroughly read the item description.

19. Don't get emotional when bidding. It is all right to lose an auction because another item will show up if you are patient.

20. Save on shipping costs for large items by shopping locally or regionally rather than nationally.

21. Always check the seller's feedback.

22. Don't be afraid to snipe an item if you really want it.

23. Always get high ticket antiques verified and authenticated.

24. Consider using escrow for very high-priced specialty items.

25. Create Favorite Searches to save time when looking for the same item.

26. Have eBay watch for new listings and send you an email.

27. Keep all emails from the seller.

28. Only retract a bid when absolutely necessary.

Tips for Selling

29. Always include at least one picture with your auction.

30. Try to anticipate all of the questions prospective bidders may ask in your item description.

31. Read our book, *The Senior's Guide to Digital Photography*, to learn more about buying a digital camera and taking great photos.

32. Use your About Me page to promote yourself and your auctions.

33. Gain your customers trust by being personable.

34. Always publish your shipping and handling costs.

35. Clearly state your accepted payment methods.

36. Always ship with a carrier that provides a tracking method such as UPS, FedEx, or the US Postal Service.

37. Provide an alternative email address in case you have problems with your primary account.

38. Try TurboLister to spice up your auction pages.

50 TIPS FOR BUYING AND SELLING ON EBAY

39. Be professional in all conversations with your buyer.

40. Do not end an auction unless you have a good reason.

41. Open and use a PayPal account.

42. Read and re-read your item description before listing your item.

43. Whether positive, negative, or neutral, always leave professional feedback about a member.

44. Use a minimum bid amount instead of setting a Reserve Price.

45. Check your email frequently and respond promptly to bidders' questions.

46. Offer free shipping by building it into the minimum bid.

47. If your item doesn't sell, use the Relist Feature to save time, money and energy.

48. Leave Feedback only after the buyer confirms receipt of the product.

49. Be flexible on providing alternate shipping methods that better suit the buyer.

50. Invest in a decent digital camera so you can take stunning pictures of your items.